YOU CHOOSE

CAN YOU SURVIVE THE WILDERNESS

by Matt Doeden

Consultant:
Chris Laliberte
Director of Anake Training Programs
Anake Outdoor School Coordinator
Duvall, Washington

CAPSTONE PRESS
a capstone imprint

You Choose Books are published by Capstone Press,
1710 Roe Crest Drive, North Mankato, Minnesota 56003.
www.capstonepub.com

Library of Congress Cataloging-in-Publication Data
Doeden, Matt.
  Can you survive the wilderness : an interactive survival adventure / by Matt Doeden.
      p. cm. — (You choose. survival)
  Includes bibliographical references and index.
  Summary: "Describes the fight for survival while exploring wilderness
regions"—Provided by publisher.
  ISBN 978-1-4296-7542-0 (library binding)
  ISBN 978-1-4296-7996-1 (paperback)
  1. Wilderness survival—Juvenile literature. I. Title. II. Series.
  GV200.5.D646 2012
  613.69—dc23
                                                          2011035745

Editorial Credits

Angie Kaelberer, editor; Gene Bentdahl, designer; Eric Gohl, media researcher;
  Laura Manthe, production specialist

Photo Credits

Alamy: Mira, 94, WorldFoto, 102; Capstone Studio: Karon Dubke, Cover; Getty
Images: Andy Crawford, 8, Rich Reid, 91; iStockphoto: Ida Jarosova, 40, Jan Rihak, 45,
Robert Koopmans, 86; National Geographic Creative: Gordon Wiltsie, 104; Newscom:
DanitaDelimont.com/David Svilar, 6, 70, DanitaDelimont.com/David Wall, 57,
DanitaDelimont.com/James Kay, 100; Shutterstock: Donna Smith Photography, 62,
Houshmand Rabbani, 48, IDAK, 14, 17, Joshua Stanley, 52, Kane513, 26, Lindsay
Douglas, 92, MaxFX, 10, Michael Klenetsky, 37, Sam Tinson, 68, weknow, 77;
Wikipedia: Walter Siegmund, 79

TABLE OF CONTENTS

About Your Adventure...................................... 5

Chapter 1
The Great Wilderness 7

Chapter 2
Alone in Alaska 11

Chapter 3
Surviving Down Under...................................41

Chapter 4
Lost in the Cascades 71

Chapter 5
Surviving the Wilderness 101

Real Survivors 106
Survival Quiz 108
Read More 109
Internet Sites 109
Glossary...110
Bibliography..111
Index...112

About Your
ADVENTURE

YOU are lost in the wilderness. Predators roam through the forest. Hot days and cold nights will test your strength. High cliffs, rushing rivers, and deep gorges will block your way. Any wrong decision could be your last.

How will you survive? In this book you'll deal with extreme survival situations. You'll explore how the knowledge you have and the choices you make can mean the difference between life and death. Chapter One sets the scene. Then you choose which path to read. Follow the directions at the bottom of each page. The choices you make will change your outcome. After you finish one path, go back and read the others for new perspectives and more adventures.

YOU CHOOSE the path you take through your adventure.

Exploring the wilderness can be fun if you are prepared.

CHAPTER 1

The Great Wilderness

Do you have what it takes to survive in the wilderness? Far from civilization, everything changes. You can't go to the grocery store or fast-food restaurant to pick up a meal. If you're hurt, a doctor isn't just a phone call away. If you're cold, you can't just turn up the heat. Even finding safe water to drink can be a challenge.

Bears, cougars, and other predators can kill you. Poisonous plants can be just as deadly. But the wilderness also provides ways to survive. Catching fish and small game can keep you alive. Many plants are safe to eat—if you know what they are.

Turn the page.

A survival kit can help make the difference between life and death.

Being lost or stranded in the wilderness will test both your strength and your intelligence. How will you find food? How can you get the attention of rescue aircraft? What would you do if you were staring down the jaws of a hungry predator?

It won't be easy, but if you stay calm and make good choices, you might be able to get out alive. Are you ready to find out whether you have what it takes?

To see if you can survive the Alaskan wilderness, turn to page **11**.

To take your chances in the forests of southeastern Australia, turn to page **41**.

To try to make it out of the forests of the Cascade Mountains, turn to page **71**.

The Alaska Range stretches 400 miles through southern Alaska.

CHAPTER 2

Alone in Alaska

As you watch the August sun dip behind the high mountains of the Alaska Range, you are filled with worry. You were supposed to spend two nights alone in the Alaskan wilderness before being picked up by a small plane. At the time it seemed like a great way to challenge yourself and your survival skills.

But now you realize that coming out here alone was a big mistake. Two days has stretched to five days, and what few supplies you brought with you have run out. And it seems that no one is coming. Your family and friends know you were headed for a solo retreat, but they don't know exactly where.

Turn the page.

Have you been forgotten? Lost in a shuffle of paperwork? Did something happen to the pilot who brought you out here? That idea is terrifying. The pilot is the only other person who knows exactly where you are. Your family and friends knew only that you were coming to Alaska.

Your food and fresh water may be gone, but you came prepared. Your heavy backpack contains a warm sleeping bag and a small fold-up tent. You've got warm clothes, a pocketknife, and a piece of flint to start fires. What you don't have is a cell phone, radio, or any other way to call for help. You're on your own, and it's becoming clear that rescue might not be coming any time soon. Civilization may be dozens of miles away or more. This isn't a bad place to survive. You've got a lake full of fresh water, plenty of wood for fire, and lots of wildlife.

It's also the last place anyone saw you. But if no one knows where to look, there's no guessing how long it might take before you'll be found here.

It's time to decide—do you wait for rescue here? Or is it time to strike out into the wilderness in search of help?

To camp here and wait for rescue, turn to page **14**.

To strike out in search of help, turn to page **16**.

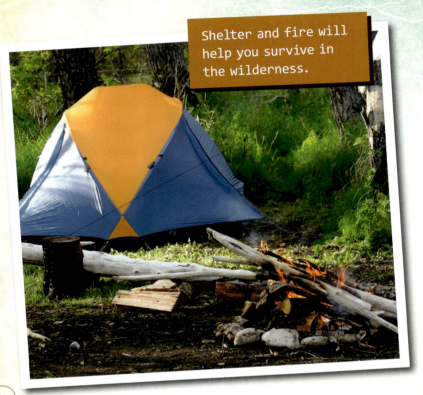

Shelter and fire will help you survive in the wilderness.

Alaska is a huge, wild place. You don't even know which direction to go to find civilization. Staying here seems like your best chance. You know how to survive. You just have to keep yourself alive until someone finds you.

The good news is that you already have a start on a camp here. Your tent is set up and you've built a fire ring out of stones. You've even got a small kettle for boiling water. And you know the area a little. There are fish in the lake and wildlife in the thick forest. With some luck, you could survive months out here.

Your first concern is finding food. You could try fishing, but you'd have to make your own gear. Or you could work on building snares to catch rabbits or other small game. You know how to build a snare, but catching food this way takes lots of patience.

To fish for your supper, turn to page **17.**

To build snares, turn to page **19.**

If nobody knows where you are, you could wait here for weeks or months before rescue comes—if it comes at all. You might survive the summer, but winter would surely be the end of you. It's time to move.

You pack your things. Your backpack is heavy. Reluctantly you decide to leave your tent behind to lighten your load. You'll have your sleeping bag to keep you warm at night, and you can build shelter. You give your camp one last look and head out.

Mountains lie to your east. The land gradually slopes down to the west. You don't know where you might find civilization.

To head west away from the mountains, turn to page **22**.

To head east toward the mountains, turn to page **23**.

The steelhead trout is found in Alaska.

A small stream feeds the nearby lake, and you've seen trout swimming there. You find a strong, straight stick and use your pocketknife to whittle it to a sharp point. Soon you've got a crude fishing spear.

The creek isn't very deep, but it's moving fast. At first you try standing on the banks, but soon discover that you can't reach far enough to get to the fish. So you strip off your shoes and socks, roll up your pants, and wade in. The water is bitterly cold, but you're not giving up now.

Turn the page.

Spearing a fish proves difficult. You make several attempts, but come up empty. Things get worse when you lunge at a trout just out of reach. You lose your balance and flop into the icy cold water. The water takes your breath away. You gasp and pull yourself up. Your clothing is soaked. You shiver in the cool late afternoon breeze.

To go back to camp to dry your clothes, turn to page **28.**

To keep trying to catch fish, turn to page **29.**

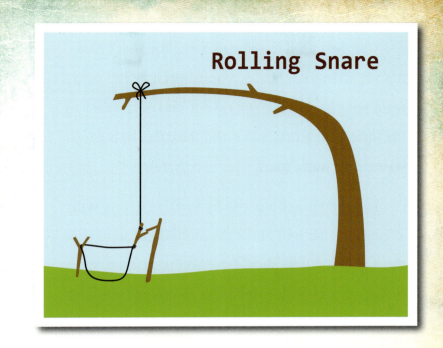

Rolling Snare

It's time to get to work on building rolling snares. You learned this skill years ago as a Scout. First you need two Y-shaped sticks. You find some sapling branches that will be perfect. You insert one Y-shaped stick into the ground with the "Y" facing the ground. You then insert the other Y-shaped stick into the first to form a trigger.

Turn the page.

You then need to set the snare. You don't have wire or string, so you use your shoelaces and cord from your backpack. You tie one end of the cord to the top of the second stick and the other to the top of a nearby sapling.

You then make a noose by forming a loop with a shoelace that will allow the animal's head to slip through but not its shoulders. You place another Y-shaped stick inside the noose to hold it open and tie the other end of the lace to the trigger. When an animal slips into the noose, the trigger will tighten. The noose will pull around the animal's neck and throw the animal into the air, so it can't escape. You make another snare farther along the trail, draping leaves over your work for camouflage.

You spend a hungry night huddled in your sleeping bag. The next morning you eagerly go out to see if your snares have worked.

The first snare is empty. As you head to the second snare, you notice movement out of the corner of your eye. It's two small grizzly bear cubs! You guess they're only about 6 months old. One notices you, but they don't seem too bothered by your presence. You realize what a rare chance this is to see them in the wild.

To move in for a closer look at the cubs, turn to page **25.**

To turn around and move away, turn to page **26.**

You head west, away from the mountains. You know that in a survival situation, it's usually best to head downhill. Higher elevations will be colder and will support less wildlife. And people tend to settle at lower elevations.

You hike for several days. Your progress is slow but steady. At night you stop, build a small lean-to shelter with branches and leaves, and start a small campfire. You eat berries and insects. Eating bugs is gross, but most are plentiful, safe, and loaded with protein.

Late on your third day of hiking, you stop suddenly in your tracks. Ahead of you stands an enormous grizzly bear, and it's staring right at you. The bear takes a step in your direction. You have to act quickly!

To stand your ground, turn to page 35.

To run from the bear, turn to page 39.

You strike out toward the mountains. Your progress is slow. You hike until late afternoon and then set up a camp. You build a simple lean-to shelter against a large boulder. You start by leaning a dozen sturdy branches against the rock face. Next you pile smaller branches, twigs, and leaves on top. These will help keep some heat in the shelter and will keep you dry if it rains.

After the work of building your shelter, you don't have time to hunt or fish for food. You end up foraging for insects. The forest floor provides plenty of ants and grubs to keep you going. Eating them is pretty gross, but it's better than starving.

Day after day, you repeat this routine, covering ground and searching for signs of people. But even with your diet of insects, you're growing thinner and weaker every day. As you gain elevation, foraging for food becomes harder and harder.

Turn the page.

You're just about ready to turn around and go back toward lower ground when you hear the sound of an airplane above you. It might be part of a rescue effort! You have to get the pilot's attention. You could build a signal fire, but that would take some time. Or you could find a clearing and try to get the pilot's attention by waving your arms and shouting.

To build a signal fire, turn to page **31.**

To find a clearing, turn to page **33.**

You may never get a chance like this again. Slowly you take a few steps toward the cubs, and then a few more. The cubs still don't seem alarmed. You smile as you watch them clumsily wrestle with each other.

Suddenly, you hear a loud crashing noise coming toward you. You turn and see a huge grizzly charging at you! You realize that it's the cubs' mother. You freeze for a moment, terrified. You know you've made a critical mistake. No one should ever get between a mother bear and her cubs!

Turn to page **39.**

Most adult grizzly bears weigh between 350 and 900 pounds.

As interesting as the cubs may be, you know that you're already too close. The mother bear can't be far away, and you don't want her to discover you near her cubs! You move away, shouting and waving your arms as you move. You know this is a good way to let a bear know you're nearby—nobody wants to surprise a 500-pound predator!

Your heart is racing as you take a long detour to your second snare. And you're in luck—your snare has caught a rabbit! You take the rabbit, reset the snare, and return to camp. That night, you enjoy a delicious meal.

Turn to page 37.

You're drenched with near-freezing water. It's critical you get warm and dry, even if it means you go hungry tonight. You hurry back to camp and strip off your wet clothes. You quickly build a small fire and huddle close to it. Slowly the warmth stops your shivering, and soon you climb into your sleeping bag for the night. Tomorrow you'll try fishing again. Maybe you'll set up snares as well.

Turn to page 37.

You try to ignore your shivering and get back to work, but you still can't catch anything. It's hard to keep your hand steady because you're shivering so much. Soon you can't even feel your feet because they're so cold. After another hour of trying, you know you have to head back. You're so cold, and all you want to do is warm up by a fire.

When you get back to camp, you're shivering violently. You try to start a fire, but your fingers are too numb and clumsy. Desperate to warm up, you climb into your sleeping bag. But that's not the answer. It's a long, miserable night. With no fire and the cool Alaska night, your body just continues to lose heat. To make matters worse, you haven't eaten all day and your body is low on energy.

Turn the page.

By morning you're in the grip of severe hypothermia. You're not even shivering anymore—a very bad sign. You know you should do something, but your mind is cloudy and confused. You can't even make a decision. So you just stay there in your sleeping bag. Soon even breathing is a struggle. You drift in and out of consciousness. One of these times, you know, you won't wake up again. You've failed in your attempt to survive the harsh Alaskan wilderness.

THE END

To follow another path, turn to page 9.
To read the conclusion, turn to page 101.

A signal fire is your best chance, even if it takes some time. You quickly gather small branches and dry grass for tinder. You strike your flint against a rock for a spark, and the tinder catches fire. As the fire burns, you add larger and larger sticks. You keep anxiously looking up into the sky for the plane. It's still there, but you know your time is running out fast.

Next you add wet wood and leaves to the fire. These wet materials will give off huge amounts of smoke as they burn. By now 15 minutes have passed since you spied the plane. You can't see or hear it anymore. Your fire begins to release a tower of smoke into the sky, but is it too late?

Just then you hear the plane again. It passes overhead, turns, and passes again. This time it dips one of its wings toward you—the universal signal that you've been seen. You raise your arms in the sky and shout with joy. You're going to live!

Turn the page.

Even though there's no place for the plane to land here, you know a rescue helicopter will be on its way soon. All you have to do is wait. Your adventure in the Alaskan wilderness will be over soon.

THE END

To follow another path, turn to page 9.
To read the conclusion, turn to page 101.

You rush to a small clearing nearby. You shout and jump and wave, doing everything you can think of to get the pilot's attention. But it doesn't work. You realize that from the pilot's vantage point, you're nothing but a speck. Soon the plane is gone. You break down in tears as you realize you've missed a great chance at rescue.

You can't keep climbing, so you turn around. Soon it feels as if you're just wandering aimlessly around the wilderness. Your hunger grows and grows. You're getting weak.

A few days later you stumble over an exposed root, badly twisting your ankle. You can barely put any weight on it. You can no longer find food or water. It's hard to even gather enough wood for a fire.

Turn the page.

You linger there for days. But with each day, your hopes of rescue grow dimmer. Help isn't coming, and you can't survive much longer. With a tear, you think of your family and friends. You're sorry that they may never know what happened to you.

THE END

To follow another path, turn to page 9.
To read the conclusion, turn to page 101.

Running is the worst thing you could do. A bear's instinct is to chase something that runs away. Because grizzlies have poor eyesight, the bear might not realize that you aren't an animal. You need to let it know that you're a human and that you pose it no threat.

Your heart is pounding, but you spread your arms to make yourself look larger as you speak to the grizzly in a calm, clear voice. "I'm sorry I bothered you," you say. "I'll be leaving now." You slowly start to back away without making eye contact. The grizzly seems to hesitate. Then it turns and wanders off in the opposite direction.

With a deep sigh of relief, you relax. That was a close one. That night you make sure to set up camp far away from where you had your bear encounter.

Two days later you come across a small road. It's the first sign of civilization you've seen! You follow the road for most of the morning.

Turn the page.

Around noon you hear the sounds of a vehicle. A pickup truck rumbles around a bend. You wave at it, and it slows down.

"Help!" you shout. "I need help!"

A man and a young boy step out to help you. "I'm Marvin," the man says. "This is my grandson, Mitchell. We were out hunting. How'd you get out here all by yourself?"

Marvin and Mitchell are fascinated as you tell them your tale. "Come on," Marvin says. "We've got a hunting lodge near here. Let's get you some food and a fire. You can use our cell phone to call your family."

You breathe a sigh of relief and thank your rescuers. You're going to be OK.

THE END

To follow another path, turn to page 9.
To read the conclusion, turn to page 101.

Thick forests can make wilderness rescues difficult.

Over the next week, you sharpen your survival skills. You trap several rabbits, and you even manage to spear a few fish. You build another fire pit far from camp and prepare your food there. You know that you're less likely to attract bears that way.

Then one day you hear a buzzing sound in the distance. It's a small airplane! You quickly build as large a fire as you can. You pile wet wood and leaves onto the fire, knowing they'll produce large amounts of smoke.

Turn the page.

Over the next hour, the plane reappears several times. It seems as if it might be a search plane looking for you!

The smoke from your fire does its job. You watch as the plane turns in your direction. It's a small seaplane that can land on the nearby lake. You're waiting on shore, shouting and waving your arms. You were patient and smart, and rescue has finally arrived. You've proven yourself a true outdoor survivalist.

THE END

To follow another path, turn to page 9.
To read the conclusion, turn to page 101.

Following instinct, you turn and run. You realize too late what a mistake that was. A bear's instinct is to chase something that runs. You only get a few steps away before the bear is upon you. It rises up with a terrible roar. A massive paw slams into your head and sends you crashing to the ground. The blow knocks you unconscious. That's actually a good thing for you. At least that way you don't feel anything as the grizzly mauls you.

The Alaskan wilderness is harsh and unforgiving. You have paid for your mistakes with your life.

THE END

To follow another path, turn to page 9.
To read the conclusion, turn to page 101.

The Blue Mountains get their name from a blue haze released by eucalyptus trees.

CHAPTER 3

Surviving Down Under

You're deep in the forests of Australia's Blue Mountains, and nobody knows where you are. You were planning to meet your friend Casey at a campsite later for some hardcore mountain biking. First, though, you decided to take a morning ride on your own. Now you're lost. The interesting little trail that you had been following has disappeared, and you can't find it again.

You're not too worried at first. You have your bike, and you're an expert rider. There's not much terrain you can't handle. But then your front wheel catches a rock. The bike skids out from under you, and you smash into the ground.

Turn the page.

You're just scraped and bruised, but the bike is in far worse shape. The front tire is blown out, the chain has snapped, and the rim is bent beyond repair. With the damage, the bike is worthless. That leaves you lost and alone with nothing but your feet to carry you. Not good.

You search your backpack and find a first-aid kit. You wipe down your scrapes and bandage them. As you look through the pack, you realize you're in trouble. You have a bottle of water, but no food. You've got a small tool kit, a spare inner tube for a bike tire, emergency matches, and a windbreaker jacket.

You stand and scan the horizon. To your back stand the scenic Blue Mountains. Ahead lies a thick forest, cut through with sheer cliffs and deep valleys. There's no sign of people in any direction.

With a sigh, you zip up your backpack and start hiking. You head east, knowing that the coast and civilization lie in that direction. After several hours of hiking, your stomach is growling. You can survive a long time without food, but you want to keep up your strength.

You know that the Australian wilderness contains many edible plants. But all around, you can hear a variety of birdcalls. It's nesting season, and finding eggs wouldn't be too difficult. But getting them could be dangerous.

*To forage for wild plants, turn to page **44**.*

*To try to find bird eggs, turn to page **45**.*

You keep your eyes open for plants that you know are safe to eat, including blue flax lilies and warrigal greens. You don't have much luck, though.

Your stomach is grumbling when you come across a small shrub with large clusters of green and red berries. You don't recognize the plant, but it's the closest thing to food you've seen so far.

You pluck a few of the berries and smell them. They don't have a very strong scent.

To look for something else to eat, turn to page 47.

To eat the berries, turn to page 62.

Eucalyptus trees are native to Australia and New Guinea.

Birds are plentiful in this area. And you're in luck, since most are in nesting season. You turn your eyes toward the sky and start searching tree branches for the telltale signs of a nest. It doesn't take you long to spot one sitting about halfway up a eucalyptus tree. It looks like a sturdy tree, but you know that climbing in a survival situation is always a big risk.

Turn the page.

Carefully, you work your way up the tree. You take your time, knowing that a fall here will likely cost you your life. Soon you've reached the branch that holds the nest. But from up here, it doesn't seem like a very broad branch. You don't know if it will hold your weight. You could shake the branch, but you're not sure whether the eggs would survive the fall. All your work could be for nothing.

To try shaking the branch, turn to page 48.

To move onto the branch toward the nest, turn to page 54.

No matter how hungry you are, you're not about to start eating mystery berries. That could be a one-way ticket to an early grave! You keep searching, and a few minutes later, you're rewarded. There's a ring of mushrooms under a large tree. You recognize them as saffron milk caps—an edible and nutritious species of mushroom.

You gather several handfuls of the flat, reddish mushrooms and rinse them off with a few precious drops of water from your bottle. You know they'd taste better cooked, but you don't want to waste the time and effort of building a fire. You munch them down uncooked. All that matters is that your body is getting energy from the mushrooms. You feel charged and ready to go.

Turn to page 50.

The Australian magpie can live for 25 years.

You don't trust the branch to support your weight. So instead you brace yourself against the tree's sturdy trunk and start to shake the branch. You quickly build a rhythm and soon have the end of the branch moving back and forth. Finally the nest shakes loose from the tree and tumbles to the ground. Success!

You shimmy down the tree and check the nest. Out of a total of five eggs, three are unbroken. They're good-sized eggs, possibly from an Australian magpie. They should provide you with much-needed protein and energy.

You gather wood and use your emergency matches to start a small fire. Meanwhile, you chip a small hole in the top of each egg. The hole will keep the egg from exploding as it cooks. You put out the fire and place the eggs on the edge of the hot coals. They're cooked within a few minutes. You peel off the shells and munch them down.

Turn the page.

With a little food in your stomach, you feel strong and ready to keep going. You move carefully through the thick forest. In places, you have to navigate steep drop-offs. Soon you come across a small river. You start to follow it downstream. You know that any time you're lost in the wilderness, rivers usually lead to civilization.

As you move alongside the river, the sun dips in the sky. You'll have to make camp soon. This side of the river is rocky and rough, but you notice a perfect flat location on the far side. It's not a very big river. You think it's no deeper than waist level, and the current isn't strong here. You decide to cross.

To strip off your clothes before you cross,
go to page 51.

To stay dressed for the crossing, turn to page 55.

Nights in this region can be very cold, and you don't want to face one with wet clothing. So you strip off every stitch of clothing you own and shove it all in your pack. You lift the pack high above your head and start across. You're naked except for your shoes. You leave them on because you don't want to risk cutting your feet on sharp river rocks.

The water is ice cold. It's also deeper than you expected, and soon you're nearly up to your chest. You're lucky the current isn't very strong, or you'd be swept away. You manage to make it across, but you're shivering badly. You quickly pull your clothes out of your pack and get dressed. Next you gather dry wood and start a fire. You need to get warm as fast as possible. You can't afford to get hypothermia out here.

Turn the page.

Wentworth Falls in Australia's Blue Mountains is 614 feet high.

Within a few hours, you're snoozing by the fire. Even with its warmth, it's still a long and cold night. But you make it through, and you're off again at dawn. As you continue to follow the river, you begin to hear a faint roaring, like constant thunder. Soon you see why—the river tumbles over a sheer cliff. It's one of the area's many waterfalls.

You peer over the cliff and see that it's easily a 50-foot drop. You gasp as you notice something else far in the distance—a road! If you can get down this cliff, you should be able to reach it before sunset!

*To climb down the cliff, turn to page **57**.*

*To try walking another direction, turn to page **60**.*

You're not willing to just let the nest fall to the ground after all this work. You straddle the branch and slowly make your way out. It creaks and bends a bit, but seems to be holding. Soon you're only a few feet from the nest. You peer inside it and see that it holds five eggs—an excellent meal!

You lean forward to grab the eggs. As you do, you hear a sharp CRACK. Before you realize what has happened, you're falling! The branch has broken and you're going down. It all happens so fast that you don't even have time to scream.

Several branches break your fall, but you still crash hard to the ground. You lie there a moment to catch your breath. Your leg is throbbing with pain. You try to stand, but it won't bear any weight. You're sure it's broken. You won't last long out here with a broken leg.

To work on finding shelter, turn to page 65.

To build a signal fire instead, turn to page 67.

The air already has a chill to it, and you're not about to get into the river naked. You tighten the straps on your backpack and carefully step into the water and start across. The water is so cold it takes your breath away. The water is also deeper than you expected—nearly up to your chest. At one point your toe catches a sharp rock, and you stumble. Now everything is soaked—you, your clothing, your backpack, and everything in it.

By the time you reach the other side, you're shivering. You need a fire to warm up. You gather wood, shaking your arms and legs as you move. But when you go into your pack, you find that your matches won't light. Of course—wet matches are useless. Meanwhile, your teeth are chattering. Your body is losing heat quickly. You realize that you're in terrible danger. You can't make a fire, your clothes are soaked, and the air is growing colder by the minute.

Turn the page.

You fall to the ground and curl up into a ball. You're so cold. Your breathing is becoming shallow, and your thoughts become clouded. At times you're confused about where you are and what you're doing. You think you're home in bed, and wonder why it's so cold. At other times, you know exactly where you are, but it doesn't even seem to matter anymore. In another time and place, you'd know that all of these are signs of advanced hypothermia. But now all you know is that you're desperately cold. Sometime before morning, you take your last breath.

THE END

To follow another path, turn to page 9.
To read the conclusion, turn to page 101.

Steep cliffs can be difficult for even experienced climbers.

You consider yourself an excellent climber, and you think you can handle this cliff. But with no rope, you know that one slip will leave you dead. You have to be careful.

Turn the page.

Off to one side of the river, the cliff is mostly dry. You can see exposed tree roots sticking out of it. They'll make excellent handholds and footholds. You take a deep breath and start your way down. The sound of the crashing water below is deafening, but you block it out and focus.

About half way down, a tree root snaps off in your hand. For a moment you're falling, but you somehow manage to catch yourself on another root. Your heart is racing, but you don't panic. You slowly make your way down, and finally your feet are on solid ground.

As you turn around to continue walking, your jaw drops. Two people are walking toward you.

"Hello!" they shout. "Are you OK?"

They're two sisters, Julia and Abby. They've hiked to this waterfall, but their car is parked only a few miles away.

"I'm so glad you spotted me," you say, suddenly feeling exhausted. "I don't know how much longer I could have survived out here."

Abby grabs you by the hand. "Come on," she says. "We've got food and water back at the car. Let's get you something to eat."

You close your eyes and take a deep breath. You're going to be OK.

THE END

To follow another path, turn to page 9.
To read the conclusion, turn to page 101.

You know that in a survival situation, climbing is incredibly dangerous. A fall could kill you. Even a sprained ankle could be the end of you. You'll walk parallel to the cliff and see if there's a better way down.

After several hours of hiking, you're tired and hungry. The cliff still blocks your way, and it's higher than ever. You haven't had water in hours, and you feel dehydration starting to set in. Your skin is flushed and your mouth feels as if it's full of cotton.

You force yourself to keep walking. By evening you feel awful. You are severely dehydrated. You curl up and try to get a few hours of sleep, hoping that will help. But by morning, you're completely drained. You're cold and shivering. You try to stand, but the lack of water leaves you lightheaded. You faint, bashing your head against a rock.

You're dimly aware that you're bleeding—losing more precious moisture. But at this point, you no longer really care. The wilderness of the Blue Mountains has beaten you.

THE END

To follow another path, turn to page 9.
To read the conclusion, turn to page 101.

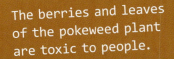
The berries and leaves of the pokeweed plant are toxic to people.

You're hungry and you'll need your strength, so you decide that it's time to take a chance. You pop a handful of the berries into your mouth. The berries are bitter and rough, with hard seeds that you have to spit out. But you figure that at least they'll give you some energy. You pick a few more bunches and force them down.

Your meal doesn't seem to do a lot for your hunger, but it's time to get moving again. So you head east, looking for a stream or river to follow, or a road that will lead to people.

After a few hours of hard hiking, you're not feeling well. You have terrible diarrhea. You're stopping every few minutes. Your stomach is doing flips, and you feel as if you might have a fever. You sit down for a moment to catch your breath, but when you stand back up, you black out and fall back down.

After a few moments, you get slowly to your feet and continue moving. You need water. The diarrhea is quickly putting you into a state of severe dehydration. You find a small stream and drink some of the water, not bothering to purify it first by boiling it. But as soon as you swallow it, your stomach churns and you vomit it all back up again.

Turn the page.

You flop down by the edge of the stream. You're exhausted. The berries you ate must have been poisonous. If you don't get medical help soon, you're going to die out here. But as you close your eyes to doze off, you know that help isn't coming.

THE END

To follow another path, turn to page 9.
To read the conclusion, turn to page 101.

Your first priority is finding shelter. Since you can't stand, your options are limited. A large fallen log lies a few hundred feet away. You drag yourself over to it.

There's a small hollow under part of the log. You climb down into the hollow. There, you'll be sheltered from the wind and at least somewhat from the rain.

Pain shoots through your leg any time you move it. So you lie still and close your eyes. All you can do is hope someone comes along.

Night comes, then morning. Your throat and mouth are bone dry. Your stomach is growling. You need food and water, but when you try to move, you almost black out from the pain. So you just lie there.

Turn the page.

By afternoon you're burning up with a fever. Your thoughts are clouded. But you know one thing. Help isn't coming. You realize sadly that this hollow isn't just your shelter. It will also be your grave.

THE END

To follow another path, turn to page 9.
To read the conclusion, turn to page 101.

You're desperate. You've got to get someone's attention fast. With no way to get either food or water, your life is now measured in days or even hours. Building a signal fire is your only hope.

It's difficult to do without the use of your leg. You manage to find a sturdy stick that you can use as a crutch. Slowly you gather materials for a fire. It's hard work, and you're sweating heavily. But soon you have a blaze going.

Next you need damp wood and leaves. These will create big plumes of smoke. You even urinate on a small pile of wood to make it wetter. Then you stack the wet wood and leaves. Slowly the smoke begins to rise. Clouds of it rise above the treetops.

For the next several hours, you feed the fire. The pain in your leg is intense, but you do your best to ignore it. Your life is on the line here.

Turn the page.

Australian park rangers sometimes patrol with dogs.

Suddenly you hear a cracking sound. Someone—or something—is coming your way. "Hello!" you shout. You're almost shocked to hear someone shout back!

A young woman in a uniform is headed your way. "Hello, I'm Mia," she says. "I'm a park ranger. I saw the smoke. Are you OK?"

"No, I'm lost and I think my leg is broken!" you answer. Mia has a radio, which she uses to call for help. "Don't worry," she tells you. "We'll get you out of here."

You know that with a broken leg, you won't be biking any time soon, but you don't care right now. As bad as things looked, you managed to survive. It'll make a great story to tell your family and friends.

THE END

To follow another path, turn to page 9.
To read the conclusion, turn to page 101.

The Cascade range stretches from northern California into Canada.

CHAPTER 4

Lost in the Cascades

You look out from your small camp, scanning the horizon. Everywhere you look you see trees and snow-capped mountains. In another time and place, you'd find the scene beautiful. But now it fills you with dread. There's no sign of civilization, and your situation is growing critical.

What started as a hiking trip with your older brother, Brandon, has gone terribly wrong. The two of you had planned a long weekend of hiking in Washington's Cascade Mountains. But yesterday you realized that you were lost. And now things are even worse—Brandon fell while climbing a rock face, badly breaking his leg. He's in terrible pain, and you don't know what to do. Your cell phones are dead, your food is almost gone, and Brandon is in shock.

Turn the page.

You're not sure how long you can survive out here. Brandon is in desperate need of medical help. His broken leg bone juts out of his skin, and he's at risk of infection. Without help, he could die out here. The thought of losing your brother has you choking up already.

But this is no time for tears. Brandon's life—and your own—depend on you. You've got to get him the help he needs.

To stay with Brandon and wait for rescue, go to page **73.**

To strike out into the wilderness in search of rescue, turn to page **75.**

Brandon is in bad shape. You don't think it's a good idea to leave him by himself. When you don't come home tomorrow, your family will start to worry. A rescue effort should be under way within a day or two. All you have to do is keep the two of you alive until then.

You build a warm fire and cover Brandon with all of the blankets you've got. You get water from a nearby stream and boil it so it's safe to drink. Then you set out to find something to eat. You're already hungry, and Brandon will need nourishment to help fight his injuries.

You spend about an hour foraging for food. As you kneel down to gather juicy Saskatoon berries, you notice movement nearby. There's a face staring out at you from the brush!

Turn the page.

Your heart races as you realize that you're looking at a cougar! And you're crouched down—the cat probably thinks you are prey. You've got to act fast!

To stand up and confront the cougar, turn to page **85**.

To curl up in a ball and play dead, turn to page **94**.

Brandon may not have more than a day or two to live. You can't afford to sit around waiting. It's time to take action. You've already got a small lean-to shelter built for him. You build him a small fire and leave him wood that he can easily reach and add to it. You fill his canteen with the last of your fresh water and give him the last of your food—two granola bars. Then you give him a hug.

"I'll be back with help," you promise.

"I won't go anywhere," Brandon jokes. He gives you a smile, although you know it's all for show.

With one last look back, you head out into the wilderness. This area is part of the North Cascades National Park, so you hope to find a park ranger or even other campers out here.

Turn the page.

You figure that the more ground you can cover, the better your chances of finding someone. So all you have along is warm clothing, a nearly empty canteen, and a lighter. By traveling light you'll be able to move faster.

The terrain is uneven and the brush is thick. Branches smack you in the face, and mosquitoes constantly pester you. But you push on. Brandon is depending on you. Finally you have to stop—the sun is setting. You find a large fallen log and get to work building a lean-to shelter. You lean a dozen large branches against the log and cover them with smaller branches and leaves. It's a quick and easy shelter, but it will protect you from wind and rain.

You get water from a small, fast-moving stream. The stream is probably from melted snow, which means drinking the water would be safe. But you don't want to take any chances. You build a small fire and boil the water inside the canteen.

A sturdy tree trunk and branches form a simple lean-to shelter.

Turn the page.

With your fire to keep you warm, you lay down on the hard ground for an uncomfortable night. In the morning your stomach wakes you up. You feel as if you're starving. Can you spend another day of hard hiking without food?

To stop to look for food, go to page **79**.

To continue searching for help, turn to page **81**.

Thimbleberries are similar to raspberries, but are larger.

You need something in your stomach if you're going to hike all day. You want to find beaked hazel shrubs that produce hazelnuts. These nuts are loaded with protein and fat.

You search for about an hour before you find a shrub with small, green hazelnut husks. The nuts won't be ripe for about another month. You sigh, realizing that you've wasted valuable time. Then you see thimbleberries. You grab a handful. They are pretty tart, but at least they fill your stomach.

Turn the page.

It's back to your hike. Early in the afternoon, you see a thin wisp of smoke rising in the distance. It could be a sign of people, so you head for it.

Soon you come to a deep, narrow gorge carved out by a small river. You have to get to the other side, but it's far too steep to climb. A tall, narrow tree has fallen over the gorge, bridging the gap. But you have no idea how strong the wood is, and it's covered with slick moss. Crossing it would be a huge risk. But it might take hours to find another way across.

To find a safer place to cross, turn to page 82.

To cross on the fallen tree, turn to page 90.

You're not about to stop to look for food. Your brother is back at camp fighting for his life, and every second is precious. So you press on, ignoring your growling stomach.

About an hour later, you come upon a river. You know that one of the best ways to find people is to follow a river downstream. But walking along the uneven riverbank will be difficult.

The forest floor is littered with fallen logs. One large log sits right alongside the riverbank. You could use it as a float, and make quick time down the river. But you know that a log isn't a very reliable flotation device, and rivers in the Cascades can be rough. The water will be bitterly cold, which could put you in danger of hypothermia.

*To continue by foot, turn to page **84**.*

*To use the log as a float, turn to page **92**.*

There's no way you'll trust that dead tree with your life. You've got to find another way. You work your way alongside the gorge until the slope becomes less steep. Finally you scramble down one side, cross the shallow river, and climb back up the other side. You're back on your way, though you've lost several hours in the process.

Late in the afternoon, you finally find what you've been looking for—other people! A group of college kids are camping. You stumble into their camp, waving your arms. "Help! I need help!" you shout.

For a moment the surprised campers just stare at you. You can't imagine how filthy and ragged you must look to them. But after a moment of shock, the kids spring into action. "Are you all right?" asks one girl as two others rush to your side.

"I'm OK, but my brother is alone and hurt out there," you reply. "I need to get him help."

"I've got a cell phone," says a boy. "I'll call for help. You just sit down and get something to eat."

Within an hour you hear the thumping blades of a helicopter in the distance. You watch anxiously as the chopper touches down to pick you up. Now you just need to get to Brandon.

Turn to page 98.

Going into the river would be a huge risk. You're not sure the added speed would be worth it. So you continue along the riverbank by foot.

You spend the entire afternoon moving along the banks. Then suddenly you hear voices! Excited, you pick up the pace and round a bend. There you see a beautiful sight—a man and a woman fly fishing in the river! You shout and wave at them. They look puzzled at first, but quickly come to help.

"My brother is hurt. He needs help fast!" you tell them.

The couple's names are Erika and Jesse. They use their cell phone to report the emergency. Then they give you much-needed food and water. Soon a helicopter arrives. There's no time to waste!

Turn to page 98.

Humans aren't normal prey for a cougar, so you need to make sure the big cat knows what you are. You stand up, grab a stick, and start shouting. The cougar pauses, looking unsure of what to do.

"Get!" you shout, swinging the stick toward the cougar. "Go away!"

To your great relief, the cougar does just that. The cat must have decided that you're more trouble than you're worth.

You start back to camp with your berries. Looks like that's all you'll have to eat. Just then, you see movement again. You gasp, hoping the cougar hasn't returned. Then you hear rustling noise and spy a ruffed grouse. Normally you wouldn't have much of a chance to catch it, but this bird has an injured leg and can't move very fast. You act quickly, grabbing a large stick.

Turn the page.

The ruffed grouse's coloring blends well with the forest.

You charge at the grouse, clubbing it unconscious with your stick. You grab it, and in one smooth motion, snap its neck. It's not a huge bird, but it will provide lots of much-needed protein.

You hurry back to camp to clean the bird. You pluck the feathers and use your knife to remove the guts. Soon the mouth-watering smell of roasting grouse fills the air. The smell even pulls Brandon out of his feverish sleep for a few minutes.

"Everything OK?" he asks hoarsely.

"Don't worry," you tell him. "I've got everything under control. Just hold on. Help will be here soon." You hand him a piece of meat.

Brandon eats a little, but not as much as you'd like. He's feverish, and he doesn't always seem to fully understand where he is. But at least he's got something in his stomach now. It's energy you both needed badly.

Once he's sleeping soundly, you curl up next to him. Your body heat will help keep you both warm through the night.

Turn the page.

The next day is rainy and seems to drag on. You build a simple shelter of large branches and brush to make sure Brandon stays warm. You collect more berries and even try fishing in a nearby stream, though without any success.

Brandon's fever is getting worse, and you're getting very worried. That night you go to bed hungry. You don't know whether Brandon will live to see another night. Rescue has to come tomorrow, or you're going to lose him.

At dawn it's decision time. Can you afford to wait any longer? If there's a rescue effort, it should be out in full force. You have to do something to get help today.

To head out in search of rescuers, go to page 89.

To build a large signal fire, turn to page 96.

You don't think you can wait any longer. You head out, determined to find help. As you hike you hear the sound of a helicopter in the distance. But you can't signal it.

Late in the afternoon, the helicopter flies almost over your head. You rush to a small clearing, snap off a long leafy branch, and wave it frantically. The pilot spots you and brings the chopper down in the clearing. You quickly hop in the passenger seat.

*Turn to page **98**.*

You don't want to waste any more time. Crossing over this fallen tree is a risk, but you've got to take risks if you're going to save Brandon.

Carefully you slide out onto the log. You lay flat, wrapping your arms and legs around it. This allows you to distribute your weight along a larger surface of the log. It's less likely to break that way.

At first everything goes smoothly. But about halfway across, you feel the log beginning to shift. You pick up your pace, but soon you hear a sickening snap ahead of you. A moment later, you're falling. The tree wasn't able to support your weight, and it broke off on the far side of the gorge!

You only fall about 20 feet, but that's more than enough. The river is only a foot or so deep, and sharp rocks lurk under its surface.

Everything happens so fast that you don't even feel your head smashing into one of the rocks. You've failed to get out of the wilderness alive, and your brother will pay the price along with you.

Make sure a tree is sturdy before using it to cross water.

THE END

To follow another path, turn to page 9.
To read the conclusion, turn to page 101.

Large rocks are dangerous obstacles in rivers and streams.

You know it's a terrible risk, but Brandon may be running out of time. You roll the log into the water and hang on. The water is so cold that it takes your breath away. But soon you're floating down the river at a fast speed. Too fast. You quickly realize that this was a mistake. The river is filled with large rocks, and the strong current makes it almost impossible to steer around them.

Just then the river narrows as it flows through a gorge. You're headed right into a huge boulder. You desperately try to shift your course, but it's no use. BAM! You slam right into the jagged edge of the rock. Pain shoots through your right leg. It feels as if the impact crushed it. You can see blood flowing into the water.

After a few minutes, you start feeling lightheaded from the blood loss and the pain. You try to cling to the log, but you're too weak. You slip into the water as you lose consciousness. You drown there in the river, never to know what became of your brother.

THE END

To follow another path, turn to page 9.
To read the conclusion, turn to page 101.

Cougars can leap 45 feet horizontally.

You curl into a tight ball and hit the ground, hoping the big cat will ignore you. But it's the wrong choice. Cougars are opportunistic predators. They usually prefer to attack easy, small targets. By curling up into a ball, you're showing the cougar that you're no threat to it.

The big cat pounces. You try to scramble to your feet and run, but it's too late. You feel sharp claws tearing your skin. Its powerful jaw closes around your throat. It's a horrible and terrifying way to die. But the saddest part is that now there's no one to help Brandon. He will surely die too.

THE END

To follow another path, turn to page 9.
To read the conclusion, turn to page 101.

A signal fire is your best chance. You find a clearing and get to work.

You start with small branches and dry leaves. You slowly add larger pieces of wood until you've got a blazing bonfire. Next you add wet wood and leaves to the blaze. These materials release huge plumes of smoke as they burn. You continue to feed the signal fire all morning.

Your work pays off. When you hear the sound of helicopter blades, you stand up and wave your arms. You've been spotted!

The chopper lands, and you lead rescue workers back to camp. They place Brandon on a stretcher and load him into the helicopter. Brandon is in a great deal of pain, but still conscious. He squeezes your hand.

"We'll get your brother the help he needs," one of the rescuers tells you. "He should pull through."

You've done it! Both of you are going to make it out of the wilderness alive.

THE END

To follow another path, turn to page 9.
To read the conclusion, turn to page 101.

You thought you knew exactly where your camp was, but everything below looks the same. The helicopter circles the area for half an hour. "Are you sure this is where you were?" the pilot asks you.

"I thought so, but maybe not," you tell him. You're close to tears by now.

"OK, let's go about 10 miles north," he replies. Almost another half-hour passes before you see a flash of color below. It's your camp!

The helicopter lands, and two emergency medical technicians rush out to tend to your brother. You watch anxiously as they lift him onto a stretcher and load him onto the helicopter.

Brandon is moaning in pain and delirious from fever. He doesn't even seem to realize that you're by his side.

You look at the EMTs. Their faces are worried. "Is he going to make it?" you ask.

"We'll get him to a hospital as fast as we can, but don't get your hopes up too high," one replies. "He's in an advanced stage of infection."

You close your eyes as you reach for Brandon's hand. After all your work to save him, you only hope that it was enough.

THE END

To follow another path, turn to page 9.
To read the conclusion, turn to page 101.

The wilderness is a beautiful place, but it can be dangerous.

CHAPTER 5

Surviving the Wilderness

It's no accident that the first part of the word wilderness is *wild*. Far from civilization, nature can be wild and unpredictable. Danger lurks around every turn. Big predators such as bears and cougars are only the start. From snakes to poisonous berries, tainted water, and bitterly cold temperatures, nature has a nearly endless number of ways to hurt or even kill you.

To make it out alive, you'll need to keep your wits about you. While it helps to have a strong, healthy body, the first and most important tool you have for survival is your mind. You'll need to use it to make the best possible decisions, and you'll need to stay under control at all times.

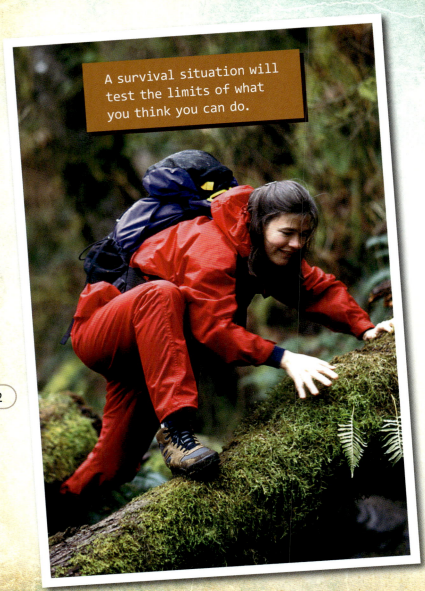

A survival situation will test the limits of what you think you can do.

Avoid panic. Stay positive. Always work toward the final goal—staying alive. Never, ever give up. The people who make it through survival situations are the ones who keep fighting and keep going no matter how bad things seem.

If you should ever find yourself lost in the wilderness, your first step is to assess the situation. Are you hurt? Are you in any immediate danger? Is there reason to believe rescuers will be looking for you? If so, will they know where to look?

Once you've answered these questions, it's time to form a plan. Is your goal to stay alive and signal rescuers, or do you need to move out and find help yourself? Do you have the water and food you need to survive, and if not, how can you get it? Finding the right answers to these questions can be the difference between life and death.

Eating bugs may seem gross, but many are good sources of protein.

People often have to do very difficult things to stay alive. Could you eat bugs for food? Could you wave and shout at a huge cougar, knowing that it was your best chance to survive? Could you keep pushing yourself to live, even when everything starts to feel hopeless?

If you can answer yes to these questions, you might have what it takes to survive a desperate situation. You might need some luck along the way, but surviving is in your mind. If you can do what needs to be done, you'll have a great chance of getting out alive.

REAL SURVIVORS

Ken Hildebrand

In 2008 Ken Hildebrand was driving an all-terrain vehicle (ATV) checking animal traps in Canada's Rocky Mountains when disaster struck. The vehicle flipped, pinning Hildebrand's leg. He spent a night trying to free himself, but couldn't. He survived by eating the rotting meat from the animals he had collected. He covered himself with the animal skins to stay warm in the cold temperatures. He collected dew and ate damp dirt for water. He even chased away coyotes by blowing on an emergency whistle. He survived 96 hours before he was rescued.

Grayson Wynne

Nine-year-old Grayson Wynne didn't panic when he got lost in 2009 after wandering away from his family's camping place in Utah's Ashley National Forest. Grayson had seen survival programs on TV and knew what to do. He took shelter under a fallen tree. He tore his yellow jacket into pieces and tied them to trees for rescuers to see. The next day he found a creek and followed it. When Grayson heard a rescue helicopter, he took one of the pieces of his jacket and waved it in the air. The rescuers spotted him and brought him to safety.

Kelly Guzman

In 2010 Kelly Guzman had planned a day trip into the Rocky Mountains of Colorado. But the trip soon turned disastrous. Her van became stuck in a remote creek, and nobody knew where she was. Guzman stayed with the van for three days. Finally she decided to try to hike to rescue. She attached a shiny foil emergency blanket to the van as a signal. She also left an arrow made of sticks to show the direction she was going. She then walked into the forest, following a rarely used logging road. About a week later, her van was spotted and rescuers tracked her down.

Rita and Albert Chretien

In 2011 Rita and Albert Chretien were driving from Canada to Las Vegas, Nevada, when they left the main road to do some sightseeing. Their van got stuck in mud near the Idaho-Nevada border. Albert headed out on foot to find rescue, but Rita stayed with the van. She carefully rationed what little food the couple had brought. She melted snow to use as drinking water. With both shelter and water, Rita managed to survive 49 days in the wilderness until hunters found her. But Albert wasn't so lucky. He was never seen again.

SURVIVAL QUIZ

1. If you encounter a grizzly bear in the wild, what's the best way to avoid an attack?
A. Run away as fast as you can.
B. Speak loudly but calmly as you slowly back away from the bear.
C. Curl up into a ball.
D. Throw food at the bear.

2. Which of the following insects are edible?
A. Grasshoppers.
B. Grubs.
C. Ants.
D. All of the above.

3. If you're lost in the wild, what is one of the best ways to find civilization?
A. Walk straight north.
B. Walk straight south.
C. Follow a river downstream.
D. Follow a river upstream.

Answers: B, D, C

READ MORE

Borgenicht, David. *The Worst-Case Scenario Survive-o-pedia: Junior Edition.* San Francisco: Chronicle Books, 2011.

Flynn, Mike. *The Ultimate Survival Guide.* London: Macmillan Children's, 2010.

O'Shei, Tim. *The World's Most Amazing Survival Stories.* Mankato, Minn.: Capstone Press, 2007.

Pipe, Jim. *Survivors: Into the Wilderness.* Redding, Conn.: Brown Bear Books, 2012.

INTERNET SITES

Use FactHound to find Internet sites related to this book. All of the sites on FactHound have been researched by our staff.

Here's all you do:
Visit *www.facthound.com*
Type in this code: 9781429675420

GLOSSARY

boulder (BOHL-dur)—a large rounded rock

camouflage (KAM-uh-flahzh)—coloring or covering that makes animals, people, and objects look like their surroundings

current (KUHR-uhnt)—the movement of water in a river or other body of water

dehydration (dee-hye-DRAY-shuhn)—a life-threatening medical condition caused by a lack of water

diarrhea (DYE-uh-ree-uh)—a condition marked by frequent, liquid bowel movements; diarrhea can result in rapid dehydration

flint (FLINT)—a hard gray rock that produces sparks when struck by metal

gorge (GORJ)—a deep river valley with steep, rocky sides

hypothermia (hye-puh-THUR-mee-uh)—a condition that occurs when a person's body temperature falls several degrees below normal

shock (SHOK)—a medical condition caused by a dangerous drop in blood pressure and flow

snare (SNAIR)—a trap for catching birds or animals

BIBLIOGRAPHY

Fears, J. Wayne. *The Complete Book of Outdoor Survival*. Iola, Wis.: Krause Publications, 1999.

Grylls, Bear. *Man vs. Wild: Survival Techniques From the Most Dangerous Places on Earth*. New York: Hyperion Books, 2008.

McNab, Chris. *Special Forces Survival Guide: Wilderness Survival Skills from the World's Most Elite Military Units*. Berkeley, Calif.: Ulysses Press, 2008.

Stroud, Les. *Survive: Essential Skills and Tactics to Get out of Anywhere—Alive*. New York: Collins, 2008.

Towell, Colin. *The Survival Handbook: Essential Skills for Outdoor Adventure*. New York: DK Pub., 2009.

INDEX

airplanes, 8, 11, 24, 31, 32, 33, 37, 38
animals
    bears, 7, 21, 22, 25, 26, 35, 37, 39, 101
    cougars, 7, 74, 85, 94–95, 101, 105
    rabbits, 15, 27, 37

birds, 43, 45
    Australian magpies, 48
    ruffed grouse, 85–87

cliffs, 42, 53, 57, 58, 60

dehydration, 60–61, 63
drinking water, 7, 12, 15, 33, 42, 47, 59, 60, 63, 65, 67, 73, 75, 76, 84, 101, 103, 106, 107

equipment
    backpacks, 12, 16, 20, 42, 43, 51, 55
    cell phones, 12, 36, 71, 83, 84
    first-aid kits, 42
    flint, 12, 31
    knives, 12, 17, 87
    matches, 42, 49, 55
    sleeping bags, 12, 16, 20, 28, 29, 30
    survival kits, 8
    tents, 12, 14, 15, 16

fishing, 7, 15, 17–18, 23, 28, 29, 37, 84, 88

helicopters, 32, 83, 84, 89, 96, 98, 106
hunting, 7, 15, 19, 20–21, 23, 27, 28, 36, 37, 85–87
hypothermia, 30, 51, 56, 81

injuries, 7, 33, 39, 41, 42, 54, 55, 60, 61, 65, 67, 69, 71, 72, 73, 91, 93, 95, 99, 101, 103, 106
insects, 22, 23, 76, 104, 105

mountains, 10, 11, 16, 22, 23, 40, 41, 42, 52, 61, 70, 71, 75, 81, 106, 107

park rangers, 68, 69, 75
plants, 7, 43, 44, 47, 62, 79
    berries, 22, 44, 47, 62, 64, 73, 79, 85, 88, 101
poisoning, 7, 63, 64, 101

rivers, 50, 51, 53, 55, 58, 63, 80, 81, 82, 84, 92–93

shelter, 14, 16, 22, 23, 65, 66, 75, 76, 77, 88, 106, 107
signal fires, 24, 31, 37, 38, 67, 96
snares, 15, 19–21, 27, 28
staying calm, 35, 101, 103, 105

waterfalls, 52, 53, 58